I0479024

River Bending

RIVER BENDING

Poems of the Delaware River and Her Tributaries

N. Thomas Johnson-Medland

RESOURCE *Publications* • Eugene, Oregon

RIVER BENDING

Copyright © 2021 N. Thomas Johnson-Medland. All rights reserved. Except for brief quotations in critical publications or reviews, no part of this book may be reproduced in any manner without prior written permission from the publisher. Write: Permissions, Wipf and Stock Publishers, 199 W. 8th Ave., Suite 3, Eugene, OR 97401.

Resource Publications
An Imprint of Wipf and Stock Publishers
199 W. 8th Ave., Suite 3
Eugene, OR 97401

www.wipfandstock.com

PAPERBACK ISBN: 978-1-6667-1493-7
HARDCOVER ISBN: 978-1-6667-1494-4
EBOOK ISBN: 978-1-6667-1495-1

AUGUST 25, 2021

For my father - Thomas Gray Medland – and all the many times we stood on waters together and apart; knowing peace would rise - if not a fish.

For all them that stand upon the banks of water – any water – and hope for something to be carried into their view that will lift them up. And pray that something is carried away from them that is weighing them down.

And, for Norman Maclean who has ruined writing about rivers and their tributaries for all of us.

"It is those we live with and love and should know who elude us. Now, nearly all those I loved and did not understand when I was young are dead, but I still reach out to them.

"Of course, now I am too old to be much of a fisherman, and now of course I usually fish the big waters alone, although some friends think I shouldn't. Like many fly fisherman in western Montana where the summer days are almost Artic like in length, I often do not start fishing until the cool of the evening. Then in the Artic half-light of the canyon, all existence fades to a being with my soul and memories and the sound of the Big Blackfoot River and a four-count rhythm and the hope that fish will rise.

"Eventually, all things merge into one, and a river runs through it. The river is cut by the world's great flood and runs over rocks from the basement of time. On some of the rocks are timeless raindrops. Under the rocks are the words, and some of the words are theirs.

"I am haunted by waters."

NORMAN MACLEAN

"A River Runs Through It"
University of Chicago press, 1976

"The river rushes
Thrashing and breathing
Thunder,
As if somewhere, someone
Tore libraries of heavy
Tomes asunder."

ABRAHAM JOSHUA HESCHEL,

translated by Zalman M. Schachter-Shalomi
"Human: God's Ineffable Name
Albion-Andalus Books, 2015

Contents

Introduction

IT CAN NEVER BE enough – anymore – to simply state that we are "haunted by waters". That is now a universal given and has been since Norman Maclean penned those immortal words. How he was able to speak magic into the heart of every human being that has adored waters, I will never know. But, at the same time, I will never have to work as hard to pen a short and eternal line (both laconic and lapidary at once) about waters that speaks to the human philosophy of, geology of, and passion for waters. That much has been done. And, that much will be unpacked for generations; never coming to an end of what that small phrase feels like and means.

When I cull through my pile of my memories for the earliest recollections of the Delaware River, I can find none from when I was a young boy. All the bodies of water in my life – until around thirteen – were streams, creeks, lakes, and the big waters of the Jersey shore. I desperately want to find a small hint or tiny flash of some memory of this river of my longing planted preternaturally under some childhood gene in my deepest me. Something that bound us together early on. But it is not there. They are not there. Anywhere.

Instead, I find hints among my teenage years. Driving along the river to go to the Pocono mountains to see our cousins. Ambling past pieces of her when going camping with the Boy Scouts at Tohickon Valley Park. Crossing over her precincts when doing the weekend circuit of flea markets in Lahaska, New Hope, and Lambertville.

The deepest mingling of self and synapses and her wetness comes when we venture just north of the Delaware Water Gap as a youth group and paddle our way down some fifteen miles of her lovely gold, green waters in a summer that holds deep mythic tales and stature shaping scenes. After that they abound.

We went tubing another five-mile stretch. Then camping along her banks, again and again and again. She tumbled into my life as a teenager and has lived with me these many years as more than river.

She is my iconic and mythic space of daily waters. Running waters. Flowing waters. Living waters. The place my heart goes to when thinking of any freshwater body of living waters. That place and the Tohickon Creek, a tributary to the Delaware.

❖ ❖ ❖ ❖

Water is a huge part of what we are as beings. We are made up of a whole mess of water. River calls out to cells in our infinitesimal selves as there is likeness of kind. We are also deeply slaked by the gulping, dousing, and suspending ourselves in water. It shudders in us and resets our humanity in a default sort of way. The pieces of us that are water are always singing lullabies to other pieces of water out there. And the visa versa is also true. Water is always serenading the droplets of you that are water. Deep calls unto deep, oceans unto droplets.

❖ ❖ ❖ ❖

We feel through the earth. We can imagine our human weather by living on her crust. Rivers can teach us to know, to sense, to overtake, to retreat, and to feel. It is in them. We must try to feel life through their grandeur and our wonder. We must learn to sense through their bends. We must teach ourselves to know through their seasons. We must simply take our task of being "haunted" by them seriously.

I know the deeper pieces of my life have called out to waters as I have stood on their edges. I have mingled with them and allowed them to define what I was feeling. They continue to resonate an ambient wholesomeness that is somehow an emotional amniotic fluid surrounding me all the time.

I really am haunted by waters. I believe you may feel the same. Wander amid the turns and windings of these poems. Find the wetness of your days.

THE POEMS

River Bending

We are not here
long enough
to watch the river
change her shape.

But she does.

I have felt it.

We can see her swell
and dry, but we do
not get to see her
curl and cut and
grow old. She is an
old thing. She goes
back a thousand,
thousand years.

We cannot see all the
changes, but we can
feel them. They are
in there.

Lateral Erosion

It's never been
enough for me
to just see the stream
at my left or my right;

to watch the river
in front of me or
behind.

It puzzles in me -
they puzzle in me -
an opening wisdom.

I have always wanted
to know where it comes
from and where it goes;
how it stretches itself
out across great sweeps
of space and where
it came from in geologic
time – from unboundedness
to here.

Where does it fit with
the roads we have made;
where does it match with
the paths of the deer?

What did it look like
when the Lenape
kneeled at her banks

and what will it look like
after the next Ice Age?
What feeds it and
what does it feed?

All of these suppose
a standing on higher
ground; both in space
and in time. A vantage
point to see the what,
and where of the
how and when.

In what age
did the side-winding
meander cut itself loose
and break out of its
lateral erosion and flood
itself straight? When were
the banks one hundred
feet further apart and how
deep was she then? Where
does the bend go before I
cross it again five miles down
the road? I can feel these
things in her and I yearn to
know more of her ways.

It is the wonder of
open spaces and the
grandeur of what may
have been; it is the awe
of what lay ahead, and
the beauty of what is.
The sacredness of waters
lay in all her drops in

place and sequence; how
she holds herself in
and against all
space and time.

It's never been
enough for me
to just see the stream
at my left or my right;

to watch the river
in front of me or

behind.

The Warming Aroma

The warming aroma
of lilac and phlox
wafted up from
the river basin;

the only place
with enough movement
to create a breeze.

The True Work of Gravity

Evaporation

is pulling
desperately
at the river;

trying with great
clumps of success

to undo
the true work

of gravity
holding her
in her courses

through the ranges
and lowlands
and time,

ancient, carving
time

to the sea.

Inference and Inuendo

It is the way
the land slopes
so swiftly up -

to the heights

in sharp and
colossal geologic
lifts -

against
all likelihood

and supposing;

innuendo and
inference of
tectonic birthing -

mountains rising
from the basin
of the valley

who tenderly sleeps
cradling the mighty,
and supple
river -

passage just another
way of writing

change upon the
surface of time.

Tributaries

Is it really that easy
for us to disregard
the glory and the beauty

that are the ancient
curving waters come
to carving and to leaving
thunderous sounds
of joyous emancipation
and subtle power in her wake?

Is it simply beyond our
caring to lift a voice and

sing of all the wonder
and the grandeur of
these sweet sisters of
the Del-a-ware that tumble
and fill her; tail-waters
unending toward the sea.

We get but one chance
and the lifetimes are many

that pay for our dank
indiscretions and
heinous degradations.
Keep their banks clean,
And keep their aquifers
as pure. Give your life
to see the slaking

awe and amazement of
that comes from
peoples yet to be.

From Penn's Sylvan Lands

It had to have
been early, that he
walked gently
the leaf covered
ground – marsh marigolds
and snowdrops sharing
an infrequent bed
along the water they
had come to know as
home. The Del-a-ware
shared the only space
they had known
with a man and a
people they did not;

no smell of
phosphates then
in her waters
that lap to this day
on the moss covered
rocks – greenish gold
in the sunlit afternoon.

The moist smell
of loam under leaf
kicked up from every
step and filled
a man with lineaments
and latitudes of his
covalent bond with and
to the land. The canopy –

a roof to tuberous growths
of sang and stretching
limbs of sassafras that
golden-ed in the
autumn letting go
of green – was a sheltering
home for deer and bear;
berries and roots, fox and
otters. Today, most know
these things as
myth or photos from
a book or label
of their consuming.
How long, just
how long can a man –
any man – stand upon
the very earth he digs
out from under? Would we
not ridicule a man like that?

How much would
it cost for us to learn
to migrate compassion from
the leaking extraction pipes
of the soul of man? Could the
seepage of understanding and
deliberation poison the waters
of the planet's skin to a positive
detriment? As crazy as this
sounds to most, should we
not be wincing at the reality
of the fracking well?

This rock has
been here too long
for me to imagine

its beginning. These
Appalachians have cut
our home in two and
risen to fall again under the
weathered weight of erosion
and tectonic debris. Billions of
years of measured change
have made and destroyed a
landscape with only wonder
as its ravishing by-product
and disease. This earth
longs for the audacity of
such a man as could leave
only awe in his wake, tender
blossoms of the Spring Beauty
under the fall of each footstep.

The earth has a way of
destroying into beauty; of
decaying into rapture. Erosion
takes what it must
to the bottoms
of the hills for
the furtive streams to
carry to the daffodils nestled
along the winding, lacy
watershed. The half-life
of a fallen tree is
seditiously displaced
by nutrients and the
alluviation of all sorts
of earth debris that
piles on over windblown
time and buries what is there
to amass pockets of oil and coal
and sediment for the great

day of mountain making
and geologic shifts of
newly discovered tectonic plates.
Our power needs are a
crumb to the monstrous
mountain passion movement
of the lithosphere; our toxic greed
is laughed at by the ability of
life to destroy and remain. Would
a man would arise that took his
place to steer us in a gentle communion
with the music of the spheres, with the
cresting of metamorphic creation,
and the undertow of natural decay.

Sing, Blue Mountain of the rain
carried across your face to the
the tributaries and the waters of
our Del-a-ware. Sing, Hawk Mountain
of the feathers cutting wind across
the tree tops on your soil, mid-air
on their dancing flight of
mating and migration.
Sing, Susquehanna
as the shallows gurgle slowly
over stone at the bottom of
ridges formed in Alleghenian
orogeny. Sing, land
of ancient rivers of
the world; sing, land
of ancient mountains. Call
for the coming of a people
that know the beauty of what
they have. Call for the coming
of leaders who lead toward
healing. When the Ravens

cry at the capital and are fed, when
deer find grass among the Outlets,
then will we have found a peace
with the dirt on which we stand.
The dirt from which
we are composed and
do return.

How long, just
how long can a man –
any man – stand upon
the very earth he digs
out from under? Would we
not ridicule a man like that?

It had to have
been early, that he
walked gently
the leaf covered
ground – marsh marigolds
and snowdrops sharing
an infrequent bed
along the water they
had come to know as
home. The Del-a-ware
shared the only space
they had known
with a man and a
people they did not;

no smell of
phosphates then
in her waters
that lap to this day
on the moss covered
rocks – greenish gold

in the sunlit afternoon.

The moist smell

of loam under leaf
kicked up from every
step and filled
a man with lineaments
and latitudes of his
covalent bond with and
to the land. The canopy –
a roof to tuberous growths
of sang and stretching
limbs of sassafras that
golden-ed in the
autumn letting go
of green – was a sheltering
home for deer and bear;
berries and roots, fox and
otters. Sing again
eagle, sing again hawk.
Drown out the gasping
of our greed.

Bring us back
to ourselves

we are not
so far gone

that we cannot
return.

Bring us back
to ourselves.

This Oxbow Lake

This oxbow lake
of midlife is cut
off from
the full meander of
my days across this
earth-place.

Nutrients remain.
Gathered
from the countless
sloughing-offs of
their origins
far and away
in the collected-ness of
who I have been.
A childhood
memory of learning
to write my name
on the back of a
double blue card
from Candyland
having seeped into
the rock over which the
streaming of my pieces
have flowed. An amble
along the cornfield
in the mid-winter
morning of my high school
days of trapping
is drawn up into the
tree trunk that sits

just at the water's edge.

But the whole of the water
is left to less than
it has been
by the rushing flood
of constant change
calling me away
from the well worn
bed of my days.

There is a circuitousness
to the love between geology
and our souls. A way
we come full round to seeing
what and where we have been
and how we have become.

What moves beyond
and what remains
has been a question
that is given up
over and over throughout
the lives of humankind.

A flood pushes through
a sidewinding branch,
carving new routines
into the foundation of
our bedrock. A handful
of things are left here,
but most are gone.

Who is the who
that is left behind?
A leaf floats across

the surface of the
river and is lodged
along the red clay
silt packed together
as a berm on the edges
of this water-course.
Tomorrow it shall
become dirt, too.
Who is the who
that determines meaning
as we shift and change
and idle in our banks
of the water of our days?

This oxbow lake
of midlife is cut
off from
the full meander of
my days across this
earth-place.

Nutrients remain.
Gathered
from the countless
sloughing-offs of
their origins
far and away
in the collected-ness of
who I have been.

Ancestral Pull

There are portions
of our days on this

earth-place in which

we return to the
streams of our beginnings.

Pushing hard against
the current of history
and the forces of innuendo
and ash.

Salmon taught us this
way to know; this way
of intuiting and crawling
along the bottom to
our homes.

Our souls swim back
to the waters from which
they have been spawned -

endlessly. All throughout
our lives.

They jump invisibly up
along the falls of deep
resistance and heavy flow;

getting to getting back
again and again.

They march themselves
back in our ichthian bodies
in phone calls and day dreams,
in reunions and holidays,
in weddings and funerals
and more.

How many times have we
marked this passage -
feeling being
aware -

of this ancestral pull
to climb. Knowing this
ancient and lurking
passion to go back.

Back to the place
where the water smells

of the richest gravel
and our nourishment
comes in fat stored from
our time in the big waters.

Evolving back to
become what we had been

all along.

Tributaries II

Is it really that easy
for us to disregard
the glory and the beauty

that are the ancient
curving waters come
to carving and to leaving
thunderous sounds
of joyous emancipation
and subtle power in her wake?

Is it simply beyond our
caring to lift a voice and

sing of all the wonder
and the grandeur of
these sweet sisters of
the Del-a-ware that tumble
and fill her; tail-waters
unending toward the sea.

We get but one chance
and the lifetimes are many

that pay for our dank
indiscretions and
heinous degradations.
Keep their banks clean,
And keep their aquifers
as pure. Give your life
to see the slaking

awe and amazement of
that comes from

peoples yet to be.

Contentment

Is there a space in my aging
where it is an acceptable thing
to forget; a place where it is whole
to be weak, broken open, and to be undone.

Perhaps a knoll of sorts, where
it is really just fine
to be disheveled of heart.
To lay off being driven for
perfection, and to just not iron
the creases of my

life and work.

A place where vital debris

may lay hidden along
the flow of this great river

with so much washing down
her length that -

pieces

drifting off into the eddies
at the end of streams that
feed her -

quietly

without warning or fanfare.
Softly lost to her mighty flow.
But not truly lost.

A place of unperturbed repose
and unwind - a kin

to Whitman's need
to lean and loafe at ease.

It is here, in my me. In the core
of what I have built. Behind the busy
sidewalks of forward motion and
progress. It is here in the stillness
of quiet pause and hungering toward

contentment.

I think I was in my thirties when I first heard an exposition on the biblical expression "living waters". The term is meant to classify a body of water as having some flowing quality to it; movement from one place to another that keeps it from being stagnant, still, and unclean (or dead).

Geologically we would equate it with movement through and over features in nature that would keep it – the waters – regularly cleaned and routinely oxygenated. Freshened up, as it were. It might be a small spring or a tributary that feeds a larger body and eventually causes runoff or flow. The routine movement of it is what makes it living. Even if that movement is a tiny trickle. It is the movement away from and over or onward that makes it living.

Mostly the notion speaks to the ability of the water to be used for ritual bathing in the practice of the mikvah in Jewish tradition. Other cultures also share the notion of washing and cleansing of the whole person – inside and out. A way of becoming new. In many senses it images our first waters – the amniotic ocean within our mothers' wombs. Emerging from the waters is a harkening back to a more pristine state of being. Each time we rise from the mikvah it as if we are born-again.

In the mikvah, the cleansing of a person must occur in waters that do not sit still over time and collect toxins, wastes, and impurities. There is some need of movement into, and then movement away from, and eventually movement out of to carry away the imperfections and assorted bits of brokenness that come with being human. The ritual is emblematically and physically enacting the need to be made clean.

Rainwater needs to settle in a vessel to be pure, allowing the debris brought down with it to fall to the bottom. But, larger bodies of water find their purification in the abrasive action of contact with air, and stone, and vegetation. Water is made living through those abrasive actions.

Sing Glorious Waters

Sing gloriously water,
sing coldly, babbling
playfully over rocks,
heading gleefully toward
the brook and her banks.
Sing splendiferously water,
sing warmly, tugging
wonderously over feelings,
tumbling graciously toward
the soul and her heart.
Quick, quick the wind has
come to steal your awe.

Moon-Bow

There is some grief in everything;
even in the light.

A time when darkness is shrouded
by a hard glow silvery moon.

A smile in the presence of the dead.

Do we not feel a damp and subtle
angst and dissuasive play of emotion;

a simple collaboration with consent.
Slowly eroding the fullness of the dark;

light shines, with varied dappled-ness
among the tears a mourning earth sheds.

Light saturates our bones
'til gladness converts the pangs hidden behind

a gallant exposure to erosion
and all that seeks to wear us down. This
simple tableaux of diminished energy
and satisfied passivity.

The moon gives itself to the river's tears -
and darkness radiates immense and colorful
bliss.

There are pieces of our sloughed-off grief
that rise above the torrents of these waters

only to be seen prisms dancing in the moonlight.

These moon-bows hold whispers of who
we have been, traces of our me.

If you are quiet enough, you can even
hear the waters in them sing.

GOOD MORNING DAY

The earth
hardens and
turns a whiter
shade of firm
in the frozen
morning hours
along the stream.

Her waters grabbing
bits of snow from the
banks she has built
by her flow.

Purpling, the
blackberry branches
grab at me
as I walk the
trap line
of winter.

Silence is heavy
in the predawn
fields. The sun
holds herself 'til
almost all at once
she rises - hastening
slowly one ray
burst at a time.

The birds of
winter greet her
with chattered song,
and the stumps of
cornstalks crackle
beneath my boots.

Good morning, day!

If It Would Be

If it would be in winter,
wrap me up in fleece or
woven blanket and
cover me with hat and
gloves and place me
on the step in a chair
facing the sun-rise
as it snows profusely.

And if it would be in spring,
make me gently, toasty warm
and place me
in that same chair,
in the garden of daffodils
and hyacinths,
facing the noon day sun,
warm smells rising-up.

And if it would be in summer,
place me in shorts no socks
with a T-shirt and a favorite
fishing cap - in the full-sun,
in my garden of mints,
close enough to my hive
that I can watch the bees
and hear their gentle buzzing
and genuine love of pollen
and life's nectar.

And if it would be in fall,
take me yet again to the sun-rise,
but now along the banks
of my Del-a-ware.
Place me there amid gold
and burgundy sassafras, and
pluck a tender sassafras
sapling from the ground
and lay it in my hands
upon my blanketed lap,
that I may smell its rich aroma
and think of dirt and loam.

No matter the scene or the
season, the chair must be of
sumptuous wood - perhaps a
honey-toned cherry, of shaker
style with woven reeds upon
its seat. If there could be one
with arms, all the better to hold
my weakening frame. But if not,
bundle me secure with fleece
or a woven blanket of beauty and
color - much as would come
from an Appalachian holler which
rolls itself out into hills.

I have witnessed
a thousand,
thousand leavings,
and know that these
would be my four
simple guided wishes
one for each season
of the earth.

And if,
if you are able
and strong enough

to pull up chair
and sit with me,
knee to knee,
I would be
touched and adoring at
our time of softly sitting
in THE MYSTERY and
THE STILLNESS,
wrapped
in precious wonder

and in awe.

In the Quiet

It is in the quiet
of the evening
reaches

just beyond the
space where orange
and yellow light
transfix themselves

to the eye
of the soul;

just below metaphor
and simile.

That place where
all things come
to merge; the confluence
of all that is.

In that place
the heart is watered
on nuanced stillness
and awe; a grandeur
that splits open our mind
with wonder - a beauty
that pulls us in. A heart

set aside for joy;
a mind opened with
wonder.

That is the
Big Sky that
is our all.

Abide there.

The Power of the Waters

and so
the power of the
waters all around
me is calling me
to find a new way
on in life -
a way to set out
onto and into -
one as passionate
and surreal as the
sensual undercurrent
of a rushing, turbulent
stream in the mountains

sometimes hidden in
the inconspicuous holler,
sometimes clambering toward
the open sunlight on big
stones from geologic time

always pushing forward
until they are all but
dried up - and then -
a trickle to their end
power and dissipation
ramble from the same source.

The Song of What a Soul Needs

It must be planted
with a gentle, mountain
song - one from the
meadows of morning -
Copeland's Appalachian Spring.

Watered with a fine
and molecular water
splashed from a rising
Rainbow taking to
the horizoned moon -
fly just hanging on
the lip.

Nursed on routine
mouthfuls of an IPA
with aromatic hints
of an oaky bourbon.

Chest deep in waters
with no fish on,
only one perfect cast
following after another;
and the smell of a
wood fire on the wind.

The Boat – A Poem in Three Parts

BOAT I

When I am old
I should like a boat
to sand and paint
and pull through
the waves.
I will put out on the
Sea each day and
take from her the fish
she holds about my
island home.

From her place
I will do nothing.
I will not call to land
or signal to the
other boats. I will
fish and stare into
her depths and get
lost.

BOAT II

When I am old
I should like to sit
on the top of the water
in a boat I sand and paint
each year –
myself.

I can hear the Sea
call to me, "Come.
Sit. Stare. Come."

She speaks to me through
the bay that quietly receives
the waters of my river.

A fleck, a crumb
can only fall to the
surface for a second.
It is taken down on
the curl of a wave.

Pushed to the sea.
Always pushed to the sea.

She is hungry - the Sea.
She is hungry for me.

BOAT III

When I am old
I shall have a boat that
I put-out in every day.

I will bounce on waves
With little care of where
I go, but only why.

The where will not interest
Me, but THAT shall.

That I should stare deep
Into her depths and weep. That
I should find in her the tears
Of my thousands of lives,
Mingled softly and hardly
Against the other cries of
Anguish made from the bottom
Of my lives.

That a fish would be taken
I would find ok. I would
Eat her nourishment as salt
And ashes and tears and bread.

CLAMBERING TOWARD THE SILENCE

I found
a very small
piece
of myself
clambering
toward the silence
at the edges
of life –
out
along the places
where desolation
has come to be
the lay
of the land.

There should
have been
no one there;
and yet,
it was
strewn all
about with bodies
and heaps of decay.
Who knew?

I came here to
lament the lunacy
of the city –

the madness of
the dwellers of

concrete and macadam.
They have taken
to passing a motion;
taken to passing
an unbridled act
of desperation.
An act of greed,
and of planning,
and of drilling,
and of blasting away
along the
edges of my Del-a-ware –

among the basin of
our River and of
our very future and
the future of our Sister
Water.

She winds her way
along, and through
and among the land
and the villages that
have nestled themselves
on her banks
for countless ages –

Ages Unto Ages.

The echoes of the
thousand, thousand
voices
of time
carry themselves
across
her surface,

across
her skin,
across
the flesh
feeling ripples of her
dank and aroma'd shores.
First, mud,
then fish,
then shell,
then weed,
then mud, again.

Oh, my sick and
sordid love
of this ambient measure
of what it means to
be a man could soon
come to an end.
Would that others
would speak their
affair with
the earth, with
the rivers, with
the sky herself.
But, no. In the
place where silence
should tender the
art of wooing enamor-ment
it stands instead against
the affair of the soul
with matter.

What man shall stand,
what woman proclaim
the madness of greed
for more? In the end,

it shall all
be undone.
Time and the
whirling passage
of its core of
ebbing upheaval
will break apart
the matter
of who we are.
Barons will be
given to entropy
and decay as will
the pen, and heart,
and voice of this
unknown poet.

But, oh
the solemn risk we run
of coming to our
falling apart
in a wasteland of
disarray and toxic
calumny exposed.

Would we should
come undone amid
a beauty of resplendent
glee; a bliss we
follow – like a thread –
to the ground from
which we have come.

The Smoothing

There is an undoing
that is not against
the growing of
tendrils and roots.

A smoothing
of the edges of
it all.

A sloughing off of
the dead cells
of atrophy and
bitter disregard.

A convoluted
but undisguised
carrying away
of all that is
not given
to the supple
and tender warmth
of needful things.

Even the icy
river knows
the warmth
of needful things.

I watched myself
coil up around my
own gritty intolerance

of a stranger
and the path they
choose to be
their own across
this trackless
land of life.

This is not a
needful thing.

This shard
of glass
under my nail
needs gone.

The bank exposed
by the mighty torrent
seems rough
and indisposed toward
grace and the finer
things of this colossal
life of repeated and
fathomless mercy.

But time, oh the
winds and sands
of abrasive time will
smooth the jagged
edges – exposing rock
and root for the
endless eyes of our
watching. Even
against all will.

The rounding
of things makes them

less work. Sandstone
becomes easier to
look at.
We find the rest
in abraded places –

a laying aside of
our parasympathetic
drive to integrate
conflict into safety;

a downgrading
of our desire to flee.

I have seen great logs
move down and away
from their knotted nests
of chaos and upheaval
along the river's path.

Tangles beyond the
touch of understanding
have been untied;
released their way
to go into the night of
turbulent flotsam and
unleashed angst.

But then,
there is
always more.

Can I survive the
aging of my sons
without losing too,
too much of my

incomplete joy
to the worries and
woes of the subtle
dying of their youth?

Does a grizzly
grieve the innocence of the
aging of its cubs?

All at once
my wrestling
with this will end;
one strand of
it will give way
to a constant releasing
of the whole Gordian
conglomeration and mess
of emotion and desire.

I have seen it
a thousand, thousand
times against the
topography of
my own soul.

Fighting a thing –
long enough –

wearies the muscle
into a slumped
relaxation that pulls
it out and away
from the conflict.
In tiredness
it falls to the
ground as if

the battle itself
has enabled a retreat
that has saved its
life.

A soul grows
this way in
the abrading of all
it is. At the end
of the day it finds
beauty in what it
has become because it
has learned to
release its hold.
Valleys fill in,
mountains wear
down; and, the
untold process of the
Waterfall Way is
a smoothing.

Make friends with
that smoothing.

Up to My Knees in Me

There is a wearing down
that comes to my me
as I stand knee-deep
in a stream and cast out
over my right shoulder
into the deep and moving
waters. It is the wearing
down I love the most.
I release the digital
apparatus my brain has
merged with in the daily
grind of life in this modern
age of speed, agility and
robust communication. I am
set free to communicate with
my own me. My heart listens
to the structured dissolving of
my me into the nature of my
earthy wet surroundings.

I become the splash
and the ripple;
I become the hawk
and the screech.
I become the sun
and the cloud;
I become the wind
and the aroma of tall grass.

When I stand this
deep in the river I know

the place from which
the scops of old sang
their songs and lore.
Taliesin became a
trout and stag
with little effort
or suspension of
belief. You cannot
not feel yourself
take on the space
of all you feel and see.

The me I felt I
knew is not the me
I feel myself become;

you can not be a
human without losing
yourself to another
form – at least once.

Falling to the river
bed I am become the
moss and weeds gracefully
blowing in the downward
pull of the water's call and
gravity of motion.
I am the Mayfly awaiting
being consumed. I am the
quiver of the fish as it
strikes the line. These little
dyings are nothing in the
grand scheme of all I have
become; Rumi was right –
"What have I ever lost
from dying."

The sun dips
slowly behind the
stand of trees on
the far shore
and I feel the air
turn quickly toward
its falling. The night
is a ways off,
but you can feel
its steady approach.

Everything has a
rhythm to its expansion
and contraction. Can I wear
down the me I think I am
enough to feel it as the me

that is becoming?

Beautiful Land

Only give me some
space - be it ever so small -

to lay my head and ponder.

Only give me some
space - be it ever so tiny -

to sit myself and stare.

The place
where one piece of land
meets another -

ALMOST.

The space
where one mountain
reaches itself down and out

toward the upward slope of another -

ALMOST.

There is a river
there that runs between
the between of that
place.

There is an echo
there that bounces

off the mountain walls.

It is in that great space
of the between
you tilled the earthy
loam of compassion.

It is in that expansive place
of the echo
you planted tender
seedlings of giving.

The purpling shadows
of the dawn-rise mist
drape the moistening
soil and feed the
youngling trees.

The days will wear on
and it will not be long
before the trees you
have nursed offer
sheltering shade and
generative seed.

Ponder and stare

- with me -

upon the grove
you have planted;

blossom and leaf
are soon to bud.

Come into this

valley of tenderness

and gentle giving;
find repose
among the spreading
limbs and cold running
water.

This place is of your
own creating.

This space is of your
own design.

This is where you
shall find your "you".

Only give me some
space - be it ever so small -

to lay my head and ponder.

Only give me some
space - be it ever so tiny -

to sit myself and stare.

The place
where one piece of land
meets another -

ALMOST.

The space
where one mountain
reaches itself down and out

toward the upward slope of another -

ALMOST.

There is a river
there that runs between
the between of that
place.

There is an echo
there that bounces
off the mountain walls.

This beauty is yours;
this beauty is

you.

ACROSS THE RIVER - SOMEWHERE IN THE WAR
BETWEEN THE STATES

*Written at the Del-a-ware River at Washington's Crossing –
But About the Civil War

I do believe
that
as I had looked
across the river -

toward the embankment
on the other shore -

I do believe
that
I had seen
the silvery-blue
glint of steel
hidden in the
soft and simple
branches of that
shrub -

of that Missouri
gooseberry.

I know
that steel
was a piece
of the conflict;

a piece of our
fratricide;

a piece of the
war between the
States.

It hung there
still as the
fragrance of
the flowering milkweed.

The flower's sweetness
suspended in the
rising

heated moisture
of the sun on earth -

the sun on soil.

The steel suspended
on the anticipation
of the darkness
of night.

There comes a wearing
down on me; a wearing
down of waiting

for the enemy
to strike.

It is a wearing down
in my center.
It is a wearing down

in my being.

Is this how
I shall go mad;
sitting here picking out the
steel from among the
shrubs, from among the flowers.
Slowly taking away my
thoughts, my reason, my soul
- my very desire to live.

Ants carrying their eggs
away to God knows where.

This is how a river cuts deep;
this is how a rock is smoothed;

Aeons of of flooding
and glacial drag.

My grandpa told
me this would come,
if we spent too much time
facing into

the bloody
and bruised business
of fighting our own -
of killing our brothers.

Water itself can wear
things smooth. It
just takes time.

And me, here on
this side of the river; and,
perhaps

only one battlefield
away from death -
the Great Abrasion.
Me, three years
into this war, I
am worn down smooth.
This constant conflict
of fighting and death
has taken all the roughness
from the edges
of my days.

I am not here
aeons to stand the
glacial tears and torrential
floods of sand and stone
on rock and earth.

But, I am bathed in
abrasion.

And, if I live to see
an end to this bitter anguish
and everlasting conflagration,

then I
shall have no
roughness left
in me. I will only sit
and stare - hollowed
out by what this
freedom has come
down to. I will have
no words because of
all that has just

transpired.

* * *

There is a charming quality to moving water that is deeper than charm alone. The ability of water to bring things to us and carry things away. The notion that we have this conveyance in our lives is the charming part. We have a natural courier service that allows us to see new offerings that we may like to possess. Things like logs, sticks, coolers, unmoored canoes, innertubes, plywood, wheelbarrows, wicker furniture, and sometimes whole garages or sheds. The river of living water carries many things away from and yet onward and toward others. This same service will also carry things away from us as well.

Water Runs Down

Water runs down.

Everywhere
down

lower,
to the lakes,
to the creeks,
to the swamps and marshes.

From one
gathering place to
another,

the water runs down.

The dirt in the
ground is heavy with
the sound of rushing
waters.

The dirt sings
watersongs
this time of
the year.
Cold songs.
Clean songs.
Fresh songs.

Water songs.

Listen,
ever
so gently and hear
it flowing
under your feet,

under your lives.

The water that
will crack open
the daffodils,

force out the snowdrops
and trout lilies,

and awaken
the skunk cabbage

that water
has come.

Listen
to its song and
be filled with joy.

The flowers of spring
have again
begun their
returning.

We are refreshed
once more,
bathed
in the chilling cold
of the running water
and in the ocean of

buds and blossoms that
will flow

across our paths,

into our eyes,

and straight
into our hearts.

The Pearl of the Heart

Having come
to the water's
edge -

the farside
banks of the
great ocean
of days -

I have
shed all
that would
hold me back.

And climbing
down from the
heights of thought,

I have plunged into
the abyss of life
and searched

for the light
that would
rid me of
all darkness.

Hidden
deep
within the
depths of the sea

I found a shell
that was hard to
open -

my heart has
been made known -

its beauty
revealed with
the flash
of a blade.

O blessed
love,
O divine glory

the silent peace
that glows from
this jewel

has taken me across
the expanse of
days

and has enlivened
my being.

Stillness
covers me as
with a blanket.

Silence cries
out and deafens me.

O holy gem;
O priceless jewel

deliver me from
my poverty

and clothe me with
your righteousness.

I Know

I know what is
written on the underside
of the rocks.

The rocks that sit
on the bottom of the lakes,
that lay scattered
throughout the creekbeds
on all the earth.

It is stillness.
It is love.

Quietly clinging
to the surface of
the stones
stillness and love
call out to us

asking us to
take them in
make them a home
shelter them.

Can I find the
space in my ladened
heart to hold two
more things -

two things that will
set me free.

I reach into the
pool of life's
waters and I
gaze on the gifts
of the deep.

Today they are
mine.

FIND THAT PLACE

Has there ever been a place
where your soul has been safe;
a place where it may be coaxed
out of it's hiding. But safe.

A space where it may be fully
luxuriant in its reclining into leaning
and loafing itself toward grace and
the storms that gather at mid-life. But safe.

Where the word defense has no meaning.
Where others mutually guard the souls of
others that are strewn all about. But safe.

Where the soul is safe to be revealed or
exposed to the open air of day. Full sun
and full air of mid-day. Out mid-field
amid the tousled leaves of winter wheat.
Blowing wildly in the brisk,
cool spring wind. But safe.

A place close enough to shelter that it
may pull itself back inside. A night-crawler
escaping the fatal snap and singular tug of
the Robin's beak. But safe. A trout mid-river
darting to the structure at the shadow
of the hawk on water. But Safe.

Spend your days looking for that place.
Go there as oft as your longing will allow –
out in the plenaire spaces. But safe.

It is all that matters. Find that place.

Stay there until the reaper starts down
your road, and then, choose. But do not stay
away because of the fear. There is no return
from deep regret at the end. I have seen it in
the eyes of a few. Choose. But, when the gnarled,
boney finger gestures toward you, it will be too late.

In Between Places

Can you find
a stillness in the
in-between places,
the spaces where
two things just about
come together,
the amidness of
two mountains covered
in a river of journeying
time. There the
chaos must be turned
to dancing in order for
the mind to hold;
that the heart
may not lose hope.
Allow her to carry away
all that is not tectonic
and unmoved, every
valley raised up and
mountain laid low.

stillness
amid the turning world.

Silence Like Dew

There is a stillness
that is beyond wonder
and awe.

It is beyond
the beyond of all
things.

It is in that place
the heart longs
to repose -

even if for but
a moment. The
place where silence
runs stronger than
a meandering river.

The whisper of
a blade of grass in
the morning breeze
can take you there;

the grandeur of
Half-Dome at sunset
can reveal the way.

Whether by the smallest
of the small, or by the
greatest of the great;

go into that space and
find yourself a home.

It is there that
all things converge;

it is there that the
confluence of everything
rises into itself anew -
reborn.

Find that space
no matter the cost.
There, the silence is
so loud it loses
all focus and becomes
a glistening dew
on Indra's grand net
of awareness. All
things become
new again.
And again.

Not Just Myself

I am not just
who
I know myself
to be - this skin,
these bones,
these eyes.
Taliesin showed me
that.
I am the knower
of these things.

The one who
knows he is yet
become the scale
on the salmon
climbing upstream -
to become more
fish;
or the glint in
the eye of the
roebuck on the
hill
clambering higher -
to see more land.
The shimmer in
the river pool,
the pollen on
the air,
the pill-bug
breaking down the leaves.
I have been a gurggle,

a zephyr, a ray in all
the machinations
of my heart. I have
crawled, and swam, and
flitted myself into
every crenulation of
all that is. Feel the
pull of the tree
to look behind
its curve, feel
the tug of the salamander
to look up from
under loam. That
yearning tease is
to get you to
feel, beyond the
boundaries
of your skin.
You are not just
who
you know yourself
to be - this skin,
these bones,
these eyes.
You are
all of the
becomings
and transformings
you are lured into
from quasars to
quarks;
from mitochandria
to moss. Feel
from those
places
and crack open

all imagination.
It shall set
you free
from the subtle
smallness and
the tiny
benignness
of the ego that
believes it is
so large.
Step out of
your timid self
and hold-hands
with
the Knower.

A Poem is Planted

The Pre-Rain Air
The pre-rain air
is heavy-laden

with a dank
moist
mist.

The lingering aroma
of nightcrawlers
and red-shale dirt
rises
among the green
gold banks
of the Del-a-ware
River basin
as the sun
begins its
slow move toward
its setting.

It is no stretch
to close my nose
and smell the
spilled liquid deet
puddled in the
bottom of
our green metal
tackle box –

from
when
I was eight.

The deet
wafting up
and mixing with
the aroma of
nightcrawlers and
shale and murky
waters of the
Churchville Reservoir.

As then,

so now.

The Proximity of Alchemy

I have seen
how the snow
perched ever so loosely
on the top
of that branch

of the silver birch
tree

melts its way
down and under
in an instant.

Gone
and now
become.

There, in that space
of constant change
and new becoming
the bark seems
soaked dark
by the trickle of
melt from above.

I have noticed
how sometimes

things so close together

may not be similar
to each other
at all. Their
relative sameness
is transmuted into
an otherness that
gets lost in
the notion
of utility and ease.

It is our lack
of ingenuity and
clarity of observation
that ruffles our sense
of expectation and ennui.

I have seen
how the river pulls
away everything
that is not
somehow rooted
down or just
heavy enough to
hold its own against
the movement and
the current tides
of shifting light.

What we have hoped for
and expected
is really all about
the sense of need
we have for one
thing to be just like another.

An imagined
stability
that is genuinely
not there.

Nature designs uniqueness
into poles of closeness
and proximity.

A pause
at
the
end
of
a
line
to give
a sense of
understanding and
recline.

I had always thought
that the people of
my hometown had
held a sameness in
the fabric of their
meaning and degree.
But,
I find
that sameness
to be
my need
for nostalgia –

a place
where there is
relative ease, a better
life and a simple
routine.

It is a space
of longing in
all of us
to have a homeland
and heaven of
hopes. A place
to walk among
the dried and fallen
leaves of our own
imagination. Welcomed.
And, belonging.

This proximity
to alchemy;
and, the making
of things into
what we
need for them
to be
happens along
the thin line

of desire
and snow
melting
into water
along the edge
of bark on
a winter branch.

For,
how we will
find the world
melting from
snow into water
can only be uncovered
in the seeking place
of yearning hunger.

That leaf,
holding on so long

to the surface
of the ushering brook,

is lost
in an instant

when the rocky shoals of
turbulence
take it
from its throne.

Watch.
Ever-notice
how the shifting
comes
and goes.

It gives out
lessons

all day long\
for free
on how to make
the change.

It is yours
to cross the line
from this place

to that.
What meaning
will it hold?

Does the
melted snow
reach out and long
for the days it stood
atop the branch
as pack?

Do things scattered
here and there by
the rampage and
current crave to
return to the place
from which they
came un-moored?

Is it only
I – the WE of
being human –
that wishes for something
that is not here
and is not now

as if it ALONE
held the magic allure
and deep-seated freedom
of consuming release?

How we wander
looking for riches that
are truly embedded in
the soles of our
shoes;
or, just loosely
trapped
between our feet
and our socks.

The proverbial stone

in our shoe.

⁂ ⁂ ⁂

The geologic time that rivers reveal and expose is primal. Moving across the surface of both space and time, the water cuts itself down and into both. And, while it snakes across land masses, pushing silt to its edges to ensure its sidewinding turns, it will – with the occasion of great rains and or flooding – rampage itself directly down the middle of its curvaceous path, making a straight line were there had been none a moment before. It is gentle at times. It is treacherous at others. It is violent at still others.

We best get a sense of it when we can see geologic images and sketches that reveal the waters from above, from that sacred vantage point we are occasionally given to stand upon and view out from, onto all that lay in front of us. It helps to see these images and sketches over great sweeps of time to get a sense of the change that lives in them. Google "meandering river" or "sidewinding river" to get a sense of this ongoing change. Perhaps even "ox-bow lake" will help thee to see the way things come and go in riverine ways.

The movement that the waters take is not just in today's flow, but in the flow of decades and centuries and even eons. How has this feature been shaped by the abrasion of time, water, wind, erosive forces? Straight, sinuous, and meandering are simply a handful of the ways we talk about what water does to and among landforms. It really is an escapade of revelation – the studying of changes on the landscapes of our planet. The way that weather impacts matter has long been a powerful image for me of what we humans go through in our own living of our lives.

Many of the poems here will help digest the ideas, feelings, and impressions we consume and dwell among in living. How we are worn away by forces inside and out. How we change over time; one portion of our lives being more direct and straightforward and another portion meandering slowly and more "lazily" through what lay about us.

The fact of a flood can change who we are, so can the simile and metaphor of a flood. Or a drought. I hope you are haunted by these senses of who we are in our material, cognitive, spiritual, and emotional selves. We have a human geology of thought, sense, and feeling. We have a place to watch the carving out of character over the span of time by the forces of the abrasive presence in, and about, and all around us.

The first time I began to know of this human alluviation, abrasion, meandering, and sidewinding was when we lost Zoe. She was to be born in five months, but would not live to term.

My interior rivers of grief and loss slammed into my conscious, cognitive, spiritual, and emotive awareness. She had not been born yet but was removed from our lives in a rush. As we retreated to the 1740 House, along the Delaware River in Lumberville, Pennsylvania for some time away to sob and mend, and begin our grieving, it all came to me at once. My whole me was ripped open by the force of losing her.

The flood of deep loss and sorrow awakened in me an understanding of what I have since come to call the geology of the soul. We are given to know, and sense, and feel through some of the larger movements of forces on the landscape of our earth because they are similar to the same larger movements and forces that blow and wash over and in our lives as humans.

With Zoe's departure, I felt the life of a river. What had been lazily preparing for a new way of living as a father among others, was washed away in the straight and powerful flood of loss that crashed my meandering banks and cut a straight path to the sea.

There is simple truth in "being washed away by emotion." Being overcome by feeling is a thing. I wrote the poem "River Bending" that first night at the bed and breakfast, journal in hand, from the Raven's Rock Footbridge over the Delaware. I wrote it because it made sense. I wrote it because I was haunted.

I Speak Gold

I speak green
in the morning
and the day turns
a shade newer –
beyond when I
had spoken brown.

The mind turns
on the hues given
by the meaning
of the day.

The heart turns,
too on the impression
set before it -
dazzled and bejeweled
by the spoken-ness
of a thing and it's
palette of interpretation
and display.

In the early morning
pink-en-ing fog

the clouds,

they look
like mountains. They
speak my morning
into an illusory
sense

that gives me pause
to wonder what
else I may have
misconstrued - one thing

for another.

How ambient
the greening spring

and the slow rusting
movement of time
over the surface
of each leaf;

rippling endlessly
and lithely over mountains'
crenulations and valleys'
sweeping downward pull.

It all moves
toward one end;
it hangs on one
endless yearning.
It awaits that
one day,

when in the morning
I no longer speak
yellows, and oranges,
and reds.

On that day,
that one day
that spans a new and
 burgeoning aeon,

I speak gold
into the morning
and every single thing
changes - every thing.

Atoms are aglow with
a fire-building translucence
of amber burning yellow.

Ochres of vibrating
scintillators swim
into my soul through
my eyes. I feel
a gladness swell
in me that is
lost between nobility
and mirth. Walking
along the river path
enshrouded in golden
leaves –

a tunnel of light –
boring through
time in an endless
appearance of
the now.

This gold cannot last,
Walt. Robert
told us so. It is
here in earth-time
an hour at most.

But, while here,
it is pulling in gulps
of autumn light

dragging them to
the ground.
Gulps and gulps of
light line the path
and rattle as I shuffle
my way through them
in rapt conclusion.

This is where the
indolent sun
burns itself
upon the gorgeous
floods of
yellow gold.

I speak gold
and give it voice
in the air
for one
eternal
instant,

for one
eternal
now.

Our Lives Are Brindled Feeling

Our lives are brindled
shades of feeling;
our days are
mottled hues of thought.
Cascading over the
epochs of time,
stretching always out
and just beyond the
full measure of our
grasp and sight.

We are unsure of
where the river goes
beyond its turning
bend and wending
way. Spilling its
purpling muddy
courses onward.

How it will meander and
then stretch straight across
its fields of lateral erosion
and deposited debris.

We cannot know what
wind will blow just
up ahead; we cannot say
what lies in wait
at the noonday. A blast of
heat or tempest

on our face.

We can only
learn to say
how we will hold ourselves
against all that comes at us;

how we will hold ourselves
within all we will yet be glad
to know.

The rose petals
lie still
in their own
aging beauty,
fading slowly over time.

The eyes see
only this;
brittle flower flesh,
dried and gathering
the dust of death.

The heart adds
vibrant layers
to what is seen:

meaning from that day,
feeling for that "one",

a scent upon the air,
a flutter on the skin
a swirling mass of
intuition and repose.

A cavalcade of days - when
love shared love
with love and marked its
passing with flower,
stem and leaf.

Our memory holds
them fresh for just
only so long– a rough
ceramic bowl of our own
collecting. The heart
it knows another way.

Gently walk them
to the edge of the garden;

silently show them
the footfall's echo.
They will turn for you
and you will be gone,
your touch a distant
sense among it all.

Our lives are brindled
shades of feeling;

our days are
mottled hues of thought.
Cascading over the
epochs of time,
stretching always out
and just beyond the
full measure of our
grasp and sight.

We are unsure of
where the river goes
beyond its turning
bend and wending
way.
How it will meander and
then stretch straight across
its fields of lateral erosion
and deposited debris.

We cannot know what
wind will blow just
up ahead; we cannot say
what lies in wait
at the noonday.

We can only learn to say
how we will hold ourselves
against all that comes at us;

how we will hold ourselves
within all we will yet be glad
to know.

The Time It Takes to Grow a Soul

The time it takes
to grow a soul

can vary
on any given day.

A blade of grass
holds fresh dew;

a river bed
repels its wetness.

Can we measure the
cosmos with a clod of dirt?

A brown leaf blows
in the wind, sending
its rattle straight

into the heart
through the eyes
and through the ears.

A calm ripple courses
over the surface
of the imminent self;

a beacon opens a
light out onto a vista
that becomes our way home.

A river takes a bend
by a lolling force that
could free a house -
and all its belongings -
from the moorings
that held it fast.

A remembrance is
brought to the fore
of the mind;

an old impression
opens us to the familiar.

It is as if we can
never know the measurements
for the bread we bake.

Simple or grand,
the soul is built on
these moments;

and, the moments
in-between
these moments.

The force that enters
our humanness is what
shapes us and the

souls we grow.

From that land -

from that soul-scape -

we become the thing
that we have allowed
all things to make us.
What we allow says
more about our soul-self
then anything we could
pen or say with certainty.

I have heard so much
that does not match the
tenor of the reality I see
laced through life all around me.

A sunflower turns ever so
slightly in the glow of the morning
sun. Now in one place;
and, then in another.

Can it pause or take
itself in a backward glance

toward what it saw yesterday?

Can a borrowed ocean
lead us to an evasive sunset
from an earlier day?

Is the growing of a soul
always now; always here;

or, can it be from
the echoes of footfalls

and dust-covered
rose-petals of an earlier

hall we did not
choose to darken?

Alas, who can say?
A moment crashes in on us

and carries us away
to the place of our person
that we are choosing

ourselves to become.
Beauty makes all
the difference.

Where will you
allow yourself to go
to become the "I"
of all becoming, Walt?

What sultry hymn
of our drudgery will
open a place inside
to hear the worth of
the beating heart, Walt?

Can a sparrow leave us
broken to the mysteries of
the sky?

Can a mountain pass freeze
our pride and place us back
in the holler of hallowed simplicity?

The dead, Walt, the dead
know for sure. Whisper the words
into the sunrise for us;

scatter the meaning in the
desert sands.
Without the dead we would
be sore pressed to know.

The time it takes to grow a soul
is now, the place it takes to grow
a soul is here.

ONE IS ENOUGH

The principles of
abrasion are
miniscule
and often
nondescript;

flotsam and tiny
grains of sand

can easily
wear away
a mountain
of angst
and even one
of strong
and
lingering hope.

It is all
dependent on the
way you hold your
face against the
change;

the way you
lean into the newness
of each and every
increment of time –

a time that goes
on endlessly in its

devotion and focus
to carrying away
with it
pieces of the
you that
you had clearly
thought

immovable and
relentlessly
eternal.

Safe.

Solid.

Not so;
oh, not so.

It is only
one ray of
a sunbeam
that feeds
arboreal growth;

one grain
of sand
on the shore
that washes over –
always over –
the stones
smoothed in
their stillness
and sitting
on the river
basin floor;

one snaking
curve in the
ambling river
to yield itself
and all its
water
crashing; tumbling
over the edges

into places the
mind of man
had hoped and planned
it should not go.

It is in one small
instance of time;
one small
and whispered secret
of a sentence about the
full and summary
meaning of all life
and its intricacies
that little bits
of nothing
carry away the
all and everything.

It is in that
small and simple
place on
space and time
that everything
is nothing
and everything
at once.

A sassafras
creeps itself
deeper into dirt;
deeper into earth-soil
and finds contentment
in the slow moving
growth of roots
that crack a rock
with dank and loamy
root-beer aroma.

A clover rises
to the sky
showing off
its glorious purple
tendrils filled
with fragrant sweetness.

The fulcrum
of the entire cosmos
is levered against
the infinitesimal
wispiness the
soul and its
simple
ineffable nods
of the affirmative.

An "ah-ha"
can stretch
itself
into the furthest
reaches of the galaxy.
The smallest
of hands can

obscure the
greatest of mountains.

Quasars are built
on the same stardust
that supports
the data for this very
thought –

this one
right now –

and the
mitochondria
on the end of
a lash
just below
the eye.

One
is

enough.

Going In and Going Out

Passing over
and into,
beyond,

and back again –

is the movement

I make
stepping in
and stepping out

of everything that
consumes me
and I consume.

How can a step

into,

how can a step

out of
make all of the difference
between things as
seemingly far apart
as life and death –
the very beginning
and the very end.

Cross one threshold
into a vista
of the aching primordial
granite rises of Yosemite,
a thundering AWE
in the center of
your chest.

Cross another
into the ICU and
immanent death.

There are
countless
million
thresholds

and lines on
the earth that are nothing
more than entrances into
whole portions of change
and erosion in our lives.

There is no good
or bad there –
in erosion. Only moving
away from
or towards.

Learning to sense
the numerous,
transparent
shifts may help us
to take one turn
just before it is too late –

backing out of things
that do not render life.

Moving away from
that which may wear

us down - TOO –
much.

Awaken
to
the knowledge
that the
one who steps over the
threshold

and into or out
of some-new-thing
is not
the one who experiences
that thing.

Every breath
nurtures the
clarity
of change.

The bend in the
river holds no
favors for
the past.

It strips all
matter from
the shore;
all stumps,

and plants,

and the living
if they are in
the path

of its floodgates.

It is the me
that is cast
outside in the end.

The one who
experiences is
at once - in this place
and all places and can only
pulse, and pulse, and pulse.

To find
that we are
this one
is to know
the journey –
the grandest
threshold,
the transcendental
door and
immanent window.

Back and forth we pass
between inwardness
and outwardness;

between an inner
psychic wearing down

of being and
an outer geologic
abrasion of matter.
Feel

the steady force
of friction;

sense
the constant flow

of wasting away.

This is how the
stars slough life;

this is how the quasars
rebuild.

All
of this matter
and stardust

is suspended
in a ongoing passing

- this way and that.

It is all just

stuck here;
going nowhere
and back.

It is all
just

all there is.

Everything belongs.

Among the Ivory and the Lavender

In the abundance of
heavy fogged moisture

lay the overwhelming smell
of verbena and phlox.

The very air
scintillating and
alive with the ivory
and lavender hues

hidden behind
a floral aroma –
a tapestry

for the nose.

The road winds through
this place – these
places –

along the river towns
of Pennsylvania –

building up the
storehouse of pleasantries
from the onslaught of Spring.

Spring,

it creeps itself
into this
place slowly;
moving ever on
through the mountains'
alluviations and
foothills. Seeking
to inhabit the
higher places of the
river valley.

This plague of
color and
deviation
from dirt
and
bark

smites the crenelations of
these places each year.

For, this sickness;

for,
this cancerous
ravishing force of greening
newness and the bud,

I shall find a deep
seated thanks
and

praise for this.

This
is where

I
am
transformed.

Confluence

Profound joy comes
from a place where
the confluence
of the rivers come together
of love,
stillness, vast-openness,
and supple lush-growth
is able to weather and
erode the sharp-harshness
of the bedrock of our days –

the buried and upheaved
igneous, sedimentary,
and metamorphic layers,
and pockets of our lives.

When these things
wear us down over time,
we are people of sound-depth
and an inner-awe/wonder.

We marvel at the simple
preposterousness of life.

We gaze
rapt in amazement
that the world has
doorways into vistas
of ease and contentment;

places of rest where wisdom
settles in and comforts us.

The suffering that comes
from erosion produces
intense-landscapes of beauty
when we gaze out –

beyond the immediate
pain
and abrasive removal of form.

SAD OAK

I have stood here
for decades, for centuries.

I have felt that river wrap
her arms around my roots,
around this dirt
and then recoil - curving
and cutting in straight and
crooked lines.

I have watched her children
come and go. I have watched
the First People - the Lenapi -
plant fish from her banks and feed
off the wild berries that push up
on her shores. I have watched
the General and his men push
off from her edges and travel
by night to surprise their own
countrymen - foreigners all of them.

I have watched the farmers take
silt from her banks to till into
their crops, learning the craft
of fish planting from the naked ones.

I have watched the new ones
dump hot colored liquid into
her blood and make her cringe -
giving up her harvest of fish. I
have watched these new ones

tame her and prod her with
concrete and asphalt, thinking
they could persuade her from
the rising she does with such pleasure
and rhythm. I have watched
as the people have forgotten to
make offerings to her - asking
her blessing; forgetting to enter
her with love and abandon.

The turkeys, they have pulled back.
The deer have all but stopped coming.
The naked ones are gone altogether.
What will happen to her?

Of late, she does not smile
when I throw my acorns to her and
drop my leaves on her. She used to
laugh when I tickled her with my
colored and dying hair. Now she is silent
and I fear for what will come next.

My roots - my own roots - who have
clung so simply to the dirt that is
her banks, have soured. Pieces of
me die as I drink her poisoned draught.
I am dying from her, from the one
who has been my life, my sweetness,
my health. I am dying from her waters.

That she does not talk to me
has made me sad. Where has she gone?
What has become of my thunderously
tender Del-a-ware? Why does she
get so very bone dry? Why does
she not laugh as she lifts the debris

of life, carrying it to another place,
to another people?

I miss this woman, so strong
and so soft. I miss the caresses
she gave me. Her silence has
deafened me and I do not
care if I go on to see another people.
I do not care if I grow another limb.

Her silence has made me still. And,
it is not the stillness I enjoyed after our
sister wind had forced me to
swing and dance and clamber.

It is the stillness
of being ill.

I have watched so much. I have
watched too much. I too must grow
silent, grow still, grow sick
and die. My time has come and
I am sad. I do still hope that the naked ones will return. I do
still hope that someone gains their wits
and cleans up her banks and makes

her waters pure to drink – again.

How Hold the Banks

How hold the banks
the water in
when so much pulls and tears.

A'coursing, turning,
ravishing
the might carves deep the earth.

Some rock, some silt,
some dirt and soil,
all be of what is stole.

Ye banks, and braes, and
hills alike
are carried off to sea.

And every part
of soul of mine
departs the shores of me.

Just where or when
these parts a'light
will shape the shape to be.

Darkness On the Face of the Deep

It is not
the darkness
nor the Spirit
on the surface of the deep
that I fear, but the horror
of our wild consumption.

A Glossary of Rivers

Abatement, ablation, and abrasion,
aeration, affluent, and aggradation,
alluvial, anadromous, and aquifer,
augmentation, avulsion, and backwater.

Bar, barrier, and base level,
bed, bed scarp, and biota,
blowdown, bog, and brackish water,
braided channel, buffer strip, and canal.

Canopy, catchment, and channel,
closed basin, cobble, and confluence,
contaminate, contiguous habitat, and core area,
critical habitat, culvert, and cut off.

Deadman, degradation, and depletion,
discharge, ditch, and diversion,
drainage basin, dredging, and drought,
dry wash, eco-system, and effluent.

Embankment, escarpment, and enhancement,
ephemeral stream, erosion, and estuary,
eutrophic, evapotranspiration, and fill,
flash flood, floodplain, and flood stage.

Flow, fluvial, and ford,
gabion, geomorphology, and glide,
gradient, gravel, and gray water,
groundwater, groundwater table, and habitat.

Hardpan, headcut, and headwater,
hydric, hydric radius, and hyporheic zone,
impermeable channel, infiltration, and inflow,
instream flows, intermittent streams, and irrigation diversion.
Landscape diversity, landslide, and leaching,
levee, lifts and loading,
macroinvertebrate, main stem, and mean velocity,
meander, mesic, and morphology.

Natural flow, nick point, and nutrient depletion,
off-channel area, off-site enhancement, and overbank flow,
outfall, oxbow, and pathogens,
peat, percolation, and perennial streams.

Permeability, point bar, and pollutant,
pool, pool / riffle ration, and rapid,
reach, recharge basin, and reforestation,
restoration, riffle, and rift.

Riparian area, ripple, and riprap,
river reach, riverine, and rootwad,
run, run off, and salt marsh,
sand, scour, and sediment.

Sedimentation, sediment load, and seepage,
sewage, sheet erosion, and siltation,
slope, slough, and snag,
spawning, spillway, and stream.

Stream bank, stream gradient, and streambed,
substrate, suspended sediment, and swale,
tailwater, terrace, and tertiary treatment,
thalweg, tidal flats, and toe.

Torrent, transpiration, and turbidity,
unravel, velocity, and viscosity,
vortex rocks, wash, and washout,
wastewater, waterfall, and water table.
Water pollution, watershed,management, and yield,
wave attack, weep hole, and weir,
wild rivers, windfall, and windthrow.
Not simply words, but states and stages.

Has There Ever Been

Has there ever been
a time when I have gone
fishing in lake, stream,
or river – or even a pond
for that matter – that you
have not been there by
my side. But especially river.
Especially the Del-a-ware.

I know I catch your glimpse
just ever so faintly when I am
standing on the Raven's Rock
Bridge, breathing in deeply
the molecules of our Del-a ware.

Allowing the particles to enter
my eyes, and the sound bites to
flow into my ears I recognize
your hand on mine as I grip
the metal cables that hold up this
glorious suspension pathway
to Bull's Island.

I can see us both, standing along
the tiny southbound gravel shoulder
just in front of the Lumberville General
Store mixing the Carriage House Green
MAB paint to adorn the clapboard
of Gerald's establishment that points
itself toward our Del-a-ware. Working
one day for veggie chili and the next

for a mighty-thick pastrami on rye.
Friendship and familiarity giving
us the want to slather up good this
piece of our history and repose. Our
place of leaning and loafing at the
river's feet. The way you hold a
three and a half inch Purdy brush
somehow exactly the same as I.

Looking north, the riffles as
they turn the splendiferous bend,
sparkle in the mid-morning light
that comes from behind us all around.
And you say, "What a glorious thing.
Have you ever seen such a wonder,
Tommy?" And I, returning that simple
line from Bear Claw Chris Lapp
without so much as missing a single beat,
"Yeah, saw it. Right off, pilgrim."

But it has always been this way. Even
when you were still here, and I forded
the waters along her banks alone, I felt
you here. Pointing out the golden water
on this side of the rocks as the light caught
the silt that lines the bottom. Or, closing
your eyes and breathing in deeply at the
scream of the hawk as she slowly
climbed in a widening gyre above our
humbled hearts and forms below.

River and dad have been a thing.

A connection and a collection of
atoms of awe and grandeur as we sought
to live the romance of Jeremiah Johnson

as a father and a son. Every step a proud
and glorious honor to soak our feet
in her majestic wetness. How can a
river carry such immensity? How can
flowing dampness hold such solidity
of importance? Has there ever been
any place on earth that has not held
so much glory and radiance from
some father and son somewhere?
some friend and friend? Some mother
and daughter? Some Grandpa and child?

For, with your ghost so ambient
along these rocks I have come to
know, that the meaning of all our
earth-spaces are not just in their beauty
and amazement alone, but are fortified
with relevance and reverence by the
who with which we spent precious
moments in their continually hallowed
precincts. Building up myelin sheathes
of passion with each breath we added
to those ephemeral dots on the map
of our days.

You are always at our river. I thank
you for that. I hold dear the moments
I feel the gentle hand of your affirmation
lay quietly on top of mine as I reel in
the glory of time. Each time. Every time.
And, always.

Swallowing

I cannot not imagine
what the dirt would be
like without her mighty
force and form.

Could a day ever be
in which she was not
here with me on this
earth-place of my inhabiting?

Will there always be a
curve here and a widening
there along the banks that
are the edges of her skin?

Or, might our dastardly
consumption of all that lay
before us, finally slake its
heinous depths on her wetness?

Giving rise to her utter and
complete disappearance from
our sight, our hearing, our smelling,
our tasting, and our touch. Gone.

Forever gone. And we, left alone
in the subtle but all encompassing
backdraft of our swallowing all
creation down deep into out guts.

May

she rather swallow
us whole.

www.ingramcontent.com/pod-product-compliance
Lightning Source LLC
Chambersburg PA
CBHW070946200526
45161CB00001BA/7